Julie Christie

The Biography

Tim Ewbank
Stafford Hildred

16

EasyRead Large

Copyright Page from the Original Book

This second edition published in 2008 by
André Deutsch
an imprint of the
Carlton Publishing Group
20 Mortimer Street
London W1T 3JW

First published in 2000

A CIP catalogue record for this book is available from the British Library

eISBN 978 1 78012 150 5

This optimized ReadHowYouWant edition contains the complete, unabridged text of the original publisher's edition. Other aspects of the book may vary from the original edition.

TABLE OF CONTENTS

Tim: To Emma, Oliver, my mother Joy, and Carole Anne

Stafford: To Janet, Claire and Rebecca and my mother Rosemary

Acknowledgements

The authors would like to record their thanks and appreciation to all of the many people who have helped in the writing of this biography. We are particularly grateful, of course, to Julie Christie herself for living such a remarkable life. Fellow actors, writers, directors, producers and film and television executives also helped enormously but some of them prefer to remain anonymous, so we would simply like to thank them all collectively.

For their help, support, encouragement and inspiration we should also like to thank: Roy and Liz Addison, Sue and Dave Batchelor, Ruth Berry, Geoff Baker, Paul Bradley, John Burmester, Mel and Ruth Chapman, Tom and Mags Condon, Desmond Connolly, John and Wendy Dickinson, Ian Dowell, Tom Duncan, Kenneth Eastaugh, Mark Eden, Jane Ennis, Bill Eve, Mona Fahmy, Peter and Janet Garner, Rod and Joy Gilchrist, Ted Gledhill, Grimsby Town FC, David and Sally Gritten, Richard Hall, Phillip and Ann Hammond, Arthur Hull, Elizabeth Hurley, Ken Hymas, Clive Jackson, Robin Jarossi, Jerry Johns, Stan and Anna Johnston, Barry Kernon, Robert Kirby, David Knight, Fiona Knight, Ray and Janet Lewis, Hilary Mason, Aidan MacEchern, Neil Mackwood, George Mitchell, Sue Nicholls, Andrew and Angela Noone, Sally Osman, Helen and Peter Pasea, Garth and Davina Pearce, Mo Peters, Jane Phillips, Jean Platts, Liz and Rory Ramsden, Alasdair Riley, Richard Robinson, the remarkable Walter Robson, Patrick and Wendy Sandner, Barbara and Rocky Simpson-Birks, Laurie Stone, Marshall Stewart, Ken Sykes, Peter Tory, Colin Walker, Neil Wallis, Gordon Webb, Matthew Wheeler, Felicity White, John Williams, George and Lottie Wood, Jonathan Worsnop, Juliet Wright and Pauline Yates.

And a big thank-you to Tim Forrester, Deborah Waight, Louise Dixon and Claire Richardson and all at André Deutsch for their co-operation and kindness.